TODAY'S NEGRO VOICES

Edited by Beatrice M. Murphy

EBONY RHYTHM

NEGRO VOICES

TODAY'S NEGRO VOICES

AN ANTHOLOGY BY YOUNG NEGRO POETS

EDITED BY

BEATRICE M. MURPHY

JULIAN MESSNER
NEW YORK

Published simultaneously in the United States and Canada by
Julian Messner, a division of Simon & Schuster, Inc.,
1 West 39 Street, New York, N.Y. 10018. All rights reserved.

Printed in the United States of America

ISBN 0-671-32232-X Cloth Trade
ISBN 0-671-32233-8 MCE

Library of Congress Catalog Card No. 77-100568

For Annette,
Bernadette and
Marguerite—the
younger generation
in whose hands
rests the future
of America

PREFACE

The almost universal cry today is that youth has something to say and no one will listen. This anthology has been an attempt to give youth—ANY Negro youth thirty years of age and under—a forum, and a listening audience.

No attempt has been made to stifle the words or mute the voice (or, in the poets' language, the scream-m-m-m). The only taboos have been the omission of anything not in good taste; and in this regard we, and not the poets, made the decision, keeping in mind that not only our contributors, but also our potential readers, were young people. Unfortunately, this entailed, at times, the rejection of some poems of decided literary merit.

It is interesting to compare the contributions in this volume with those of Negre poets under thirty who were included in our anthology "Negro Voices," published by Henry Harrison in 1938. The first thing which is immediately evident is that today's poets are much more race oriented . . . one might even say race saturated. There is little levity—even among the youngest. There is deeper pride in race, and a determination to change the way things are. We cannot deny that there is also more militancy and more unadorned hate flowing from their pens.

But—mixed with the militancy is a poignant cry for somebody to help, and somebody to care. Barbara Baker says "Somebody please, Please help me, teach me, *Care*." Yvette Johnson says "Does anybody care?" Another poet wrote about her boat putting out to sea under the burden of living, then climbed upon a bridge and jumped to her death at the age of twenty-three.

7

We of the older generation are left with the question: What happened to OUR faith and OUR courage that we could not—or did not—pass on to our children that "something they could cling to" and come up smiling in today's troubled upside down world?

Thanks are due, first, to the publisher for suggesting the book; to the many poets—accepted and rejected—who gave us the privilege of getting to know them through their poetry. Sincere thanks are due to my friend and fellow poet, Nerissa Long Milton, who devoted hours of her leisure time to reading the poetry to me while I recuperated from eye surgery, and to doing some of the editorial chores I could not see to perform.

Thanks are due Mrs. W. Elizabeth Baltimore who typed the manuscript, and to the following for permission to reprint: To the *Negro Digest* for "A Resonant Silence" by David Llorens; to Prairie Press for excerpts from "Free Wine on Communion Day" by Linwood D. Smith, from *68 Poets;* to Nikki Giovanni for "The Funeral of Martin Luther King, Jr.," "For Saundra," "My Poem," and "Black Judgement," the title poem of her book, *Black Judgement,* from which all of her poems were reprinted; and to Carolyn M. Rodgers for "We Dance Like Ella Riffs," and "U Name This One," from her book, *Songs of a Blackbird.*

Beatrice M. Murphy

CONTENTS

9

TODAY'S
NEGRO VOICES

BARBARA ANNE BAKER

Barbara Anne Baker, twenty-nine years old, was born in Union City, Tennessee, graduated from high school there, and attended business school in Detroit, Michigan. The mother of four children, she lives in Scotland, where her husband is stationed with the United States Navy. She has been writing since she was eight years old but only recently became interested in having her work published.

"GROW IN HOPE AND GRACE"

—And you begin to grow, but no one notices—
"Don't stand in front of the T.V."
"Go to the store and get a bottle of milk."
"Does God have a mother?"
"Shut up and don't ask so many stupid questions."

And you continue to grow, and there is a feeling in you.
If you could define it the definition would be empty;
But you can't; you just moon around—
"Can't you find something to do?" Your eyes flash
A plea that says "Please help," but no one does.
Your heart aches, and you think surely you will die—
But you don't; you just continue to grow.

Now the emptiness grows with you . . . But there must be
    a way,
a means by which—but how! How! "Somebody please!
Please help me! I'll do *anything*. Just show me,
teach me, *care* somebody; please *care!*"

So you get older,
The growing has stopped both in body and mind,
and each day you sit and peer
from behind your veil of emptiness
watching life drift past.
You can never remember being a part of life,
The emptiness fills your past, your present
and stands mockingly
in the doorway of your future.

YILLIE BEY

William Manns, II (Yillie Bey), twenty-one years old is a native New Yorker. He has been writing for some time, but he considers his first big break the recent offer of an opportunity to write for a productions company founded by LeRoi Jones.

MAKING OF A MILITANT

I am an inter-citian, I am Black as you can see.
I love Black Culture, I love Black Art, and I'm as militant
as can be.
I didn't always love Black things and I was a moderate at
one time
But things started to happen that slowly blew my mind.
The transition started some years ago up in the Weequahic
section,
When a friend and I were walking, not conscious of our
direction.
We were traveling Bragaw Avenue, between Wainwright
and Schley
When from out of nowhere a cop car rolled by.
They stopped the car and beckoned us over, I could see the
anger in each face.
They called us niggers, shoved us around, and poked fun
at our race.
They asked us what we were doing up there, to which I did
reply:
Why we're just taking a walk officers, I wouldn't tell you a
lie.
They told us Black niggers didn't have no business in that
part of town
And if they ever caught us up there again we'd be six feet
underground.
That was the shake needed to remove the sand from my eyes
It was then that I began to reject and refute the whiteman's
lies.
I began to see quite clearly what the whiteman had done
for ages
Exploiting, degrading, oppressing, making US victims of his
vicious rages.
I thought about how long the Blackman had been dead
Now I was alive and to prove it, I snatched the stocking cap
from my head.

I stopped assimulating and duplicating the wicked ways of
the "west"
I began to read Malcolm, Marcus and Jones, they told me I
was best.
Now I know who I am and I know what I've got to do.
I've got to write, I've got to speak to wake up Brothers like
you.
Look out—Here I come, I'm angry, militant and mean
I'm the new breed Blackman, the kind that you've never
seen.
Look out—Here I come, blood in the eyes that once held tons
of sand
An Afro on my head and a cocktail in my hand.
Look out—it ain't the kind you drink.

DONALD E. BOGLE

Donald E. Bogle, twenty-two years old, is a native of Pennsylvania. He has received numerous awards for his writing, and a Rockefeller Foundation grant to study law. He worked in New York as production assistant and story editor for producer Otto Preminger. Presently, he is Assistant Editor of *Ebony Magazine.*

"AN ARISTOTELIAN ELEGY"

At one time
he had called himself
a poet

Art for him
was intended
(and later interpreted)
as an imitation
of reality

But now
he had his doubts

If art were
no imitation
nor even a
criticism of
that which was real

then of what would
he write

Could he create
something that
would extend
his
experience
and
their
experience, too
and if so, this then being
the new task of art,
was an extension enough

After debating

on the issue
he realized a
poet, as all
poets before
him had said,
really was a
singer of songs
because
poetry was feeling
and feeling is music
and then
he knew he was no poet
because he was no musician

no—an essayist—maybe

but a poet—no, never

NOW

now
here
at a time
when there is
not much time

to either
debate or rehearse
or even mourn

to neither
intellectualize
nor
prophesize
nor even criticize;

now
when we must
still explain,
when we must
still ask
the overwhelming question
when we still
cannot
yet be—

now
is
now
and we know
the now;
the
problem
is to know
the tomorrow

TOWNSEND T. BREWSTER

Townsend T. Brewster, twenty years old, is a student at the University of Denver. He has published both original poetry and translations.

BLACK IS BEAUTIFUL

Or so our cleaning woman tells us—
Though, as of when,
She has not specified.
A little scholarship brought to bear
May possibly throw light upon the problem
And, in consequence, its chronology.

Corneille, in the *Examen* of his *Andromede,*
Sets aside Ovid, his source,
And proves his heroine must have been white
By virtue of the fact that Perseus, being Greek,
And having a Greek eye for beauty,
Could otherwise not have loved her.

On the other hand, Ethiopian Memnon.
With his skin of polished jet,
Was one whom the Greeks themselves considered,
Along with Achilles and Idomeneus of Crete,
"The handsomest man alive."

Corneille's contemporary, Rembrandt van Rijn,
His critics, and his viewers could see a slaughtered ox
With unrevolted eyes,
Eyes, moreover, that found the unsightly
In ruins, in ragged beggars, in ramshackle hovels,
That is to say where we should discover
The picturesque.

In 1661, Rembrandt painted *Two Negroes;*
Twenty-nine years before, he had done the portrait
Of Maurits Huygens, whose physiognomy,
Though that of a Secretary of State of the Council of Holland,
Is nevertheless
Suspicious.
The crucial question, of course, is whether Rembrandt

Looked upon these subjects as
Beautiful, ugly, or picturesque.

In summation,
A sampling of attitudes
From randomly selected eras and lands,
From Greece, from Rome, from France,
And, less definitively, from Holland,
Leads us to conclude that the beauty of Blacks
(Unlike the beauty of Whites, which is absolute)
Is subject to fads and fashions.
Currently,
Black is beautiful.

THELMA PARKER COX

Thelma Parker Cox, thirty years old, is married and the mother of nine children. She has been writing since childhood but did not become interested in publication until inspired by the Freedom March on Washington in August 1963. Her husband is a Jazz musician.

EVOLUTION

Black faces lifted to the heavens . . . searching,
Black voices raised for all to hear . . . pleading,
Black souls, tired . . .
Black minds, confused . . .
Black man lost three hundred years.

Black arms chained by his oppressors,
Black legs bound to prevent escape,
Black bodies whipped . . .
Black heads bowed . . .
Black man a slave three hundred years.

Three hundred years, too long for oppression,
Three hundred years, being slaves to the whites,
Black man, awake . . .
White man, beware . . .
Black man aroused, new life he seeks.

Black man had a dream, a vision of freedom,
Black freedom now . . . tomorrow's too late,
New day has come . . .
Black man revolts . . .
Black man has rights, he wants them now.

Black arms extend, to take what's his,
Black legs stride forth, will not retreat,
Black bodies proud . . .
Black heads high . . .
Black man rebels, denied no more.

Black faces lifted to the heavens . . . protesting,
Black voices raised for all to hear . . . demanding
Black soul, restless . . .
Black minds, determined . . .
Black man free . . . Black man free . . .

FRUSTRATION, A HERITAGE

Years of frustration, of futility,
Life of a woman, black, just like me.
Seeing her husband, watching his face,
As he toils without gaining his rightful place.

No place for her husband, deaf ears to his plea,
Denied for the reason, he's black, just like me.
Though they set their goals, their standards high,
Their plans for a lifetime wither and die.

She pretends not to notice the pain that shows there,
As she watches his eyes try to hide his despair.
She nurses his children on the milk of their plans,
A vision for their future above any man's.

A future of joy, of success, and of hope,
Is not for these children, they too, must grope,
Through a life of frustration, of futility,
For they too, must pay. Since they're black, just like me.

GREGORY J. FORD

Gregory James Ford, eighteen years old, was born in Sacramento, California, and attended high school in East Palo Alto, California. Presently, he is attending St. John's College in Santa Fe, New Mexico, but has not decided definitely his future goals.

BITS AND PIECES

Freckles
tickle your nose;
even at this moment
the lisp of blonde
throws your laughter at me

and

love happens (!)

     ✿   ✿   ✿

I
dare not love you
i fear
your color
means too much
to me.

     ✿   ✿   ✿

alone . . .
unto itself
my love skims
on a crystalline sea

     ✿   ✿   ✿

tic tac
tic tac
tic . . .
tic . . . . .
tac
tic tac
your platinum heeled pause
only insures your leaving
and
though I think we loved,
somehow
I am glad.

31

NIKKI GIOVANNI

Nikki Giovanni, twenty-six years old, has written book reviews and short stories for *Negro Digest*. Her short stories are included in the anthology, *Black Creations*. She is an editor on *Onyx Magazine* and *Black Dialogue*. Two pamphlets of her poetry have been published: *Black Feeling; Black Talk,* and *Black Judgement*. A collection of her short stories will be published sometime soon.

BLACK JUDGEMENT

Sometimes we find we have nothing to give
but love
which is a poem
which I give
For the Black Revolution.

FOR SAUNDRA

i wanted to write
a poem
that rhymes
but revolution doesn't lend
itself to be-bopping

then my neighbor
who thinks i hate
asked—do you write
tree poems—i like trees
so i thought
i'll write a beautiful green tree poem
peeked from my window
to check the image
noticed the school yard was covered
with asphalt
no green—no trees grow
in manhattan

then, well, i thought the sky
i'll do a big blue sky poem
but all the clouds have winged
low since no-Dick was elected

so i thought again
and it occurred to me
maybe i shouldn't write
at all
but clean my gun
and check my kerosene supply

perhaps these are not poetic
times
at all

MY POEM

i am 25 years old
black female poet
wrote a poem asking
nigger can you kill
if they kill me
it won't stop
the revolution

i have been robbed
it looked like they knew
that i was to be hit
they took my tv
my two rings
my piece of african print
and my two guns
if they take my life
it won't stop
the revolution

my phone is tapped
my mail is opened
they've caused me to turn
on all my old friends
and all my new lovers
if i hate all black
people
and all negroes
it won't stop
the revolution

i'm afraid to tell
my roommate where i'm going
and scared to tell
people if i'm coming
if i sit here

for the rest
of my life
it won't stop
the revolution

if i never write
another poem
or short story
if i flunk out
of grad school
if my car is reclaimed
and my record player
won't play
and if i never see
a peaceful day
or do a meaningful
black thing
it won't stop
the revolution

the revolution
is in the streets
and if i stay on
the 5th floor
it will go on
if i never do
anything
it will go on

THE FUNERAL OF MARTIN LUTHER KING, JR.

His headstone said
FREE AT LAST, FREE AT LAST
But death is a slave's freedom
We seek the freedom of free men
And the construction of a world
Where Martin Luther King could have lived and preached
non-violence.

BERNETTE GOLDEN

Bernette Golden, nineteen years old, is a sophomore at American University in Washington, D. C. After college she plans to write, and teach African History—either on the college or high school level.

MORNING

Morning is a state of mind
Unfolding
With a lazy stagnant sameness
The cobweb patterns
Of yesterday's todays.

Morning is a vacant feeling
Shoving black night's
Reverie
Into the open
Arms of time.

Morning is the singular
Halting thought
Of today
And the
Invisible weight
Of things to
Come.

THERE ARE SEEDS TO SOW

Black people, arise
From those once-sealed tombs
Of mental death
Which, for too long
Have claimed
The fertility of our minds
And the humanity
Of our souls;—
There are seeds to sow.

Black people, raise
The chorus of your voices
In the funeral chant
For the nigger
And resurrect
That proud
Dark spirit
That smoulders
In the being
Of us all;—
There are seeds to sow.

Black people,
No longer shall we be
The mindless, impotent atoms
Our blood-stained past
Has forced us to become;
There are seeds to sow.

Black people, deny
That self-hating spirit,
That loveless legacy
Of soulful
Nonexistence;

And plant in the minds of
Young children
The unbridled pride
And warm sensation of human beauty.
These are the seeds to sow.

WORDS

The words that I speak
Float softly on the wind
And reach for ears
That hear me not

The pleas that I make
Drown silently
In the tears
That find no exit
From my heart

And the sound
Of a hollow laugh
Shadows the emptiness
Of myself.

ROSLYN GREER

Roslyn Greer, eighteen years old, is a native Californian. She graduated from high school in February 1969 and plans to attend Pasadena City College and major in Journalism.

TRIANGLE

Hate and love, hate and love; Circles still remain.
Love and hate, love and hate; Squares begin to frame.

Lines go up, lines go down; Hide my enter interior.
Lines go down, lines go up; Make an angled barrier.

Circle round, frame at corner, stalk a line so high.
Yet, when it comes to hate a love, sense of angle dies.

VERA E. GUERARD

Vera Elizabeth Guerard was twenty-three years old at the time of her death in late 1967. A native of Tennessee, she had been writing poetry since early childhood; and her works had been featured in books by her father, the Reverend A. L. Guerard. She was also a talented singer and made guest appearances in churches and before other religious groups.

AT SEA

My time is nearly up
Life seems done with me.
For the ship is really lost
And I shall die at sea.

It seems I can't escape
All life boats are gone.
To God I must now pray
As the future is unknown.

The ship is sinking very low
And I shall die at sea.
The God in Heaven, I hope will
remember me.

SPRING OF JOY

The sunshine after rain
Leaves my soul filled with mist
Of happiness and remembrance
When we shared our first kiss.
Only a look will fill my need
For eyes speak more than words;
I hope my eyes will say,
"You're my love bird!"
The air so clean, after a balmy wind
Leaves me rested, a contented mind.
I'm looking forward to spring
The season that cheers mankind.

VERNOY E. HITE

Vernoy Hite, nineteen years old, is a native of Los Angeles, California. He was an honor student through secondary school, and held the office of Student Body President. He is now a Sophomore at the University of California at Los Angeles.

MALCOLM X

One a valley among the peaks of humanity
Then exalted above all,
Yet able to relate to the call
Trapped by the reigns of life.
A child of the earth.

TRAPPED

The caverns of my mind are wrinkled
And heavily creased,
Time unsympathetic—the world unyielding.
My heart is too heavy to bear,
I look for a way out—
Life is inflexible.

My tormented innerisms reach out for a
Hand, a guide, a friend.
They return with more broken spirits
Than before,
Help is needed, the finding of which is
A herculean task—I am mortal,
Life is inflexible.

Let me cry, let me release the emotions—
The pressure increases.
I can't—I want to—I can't!
I am numb,
Life is inflexible.

Is there another side?
Are we all damned to anguish, mixed
Emotions, and torment? This hell!
Is there another side to the coin, or,
Is life inflexible?

MARSHA ANN JACKSON

Marsha Ann Jackson, twenty-three years old, has been interested in writing poetry since she was nine years old, and her poetry has appeared in College literary magazines. She received the New York State Regents Scholarship and the Manhattanville John La Farge Scholarship. Currently she is teaching school in Mt. Vernon, New York.

IN BETWEEN TIME
(TRANSCIENCE)

Yesterday a world was born.
    Tomorrow, it shall die.
All living's in between time.

Yesterday a world of worms,
    Tomorrow, dead, dry crow's feed,
But as for today, the butterfly
    Rules the world as king.

Yesterday a fly-speck egg,
    Tomorrow, food for maggots,
        But, ah, today,
    A breath of God
        On man-legs
Holds eternity in his hands
    And molds new worlds
        from decay
In the living done
    Between time.

TEARS AND A DREAM

My soul
    cried out to you
        for comfort,
for I was afraid—
    and you turned me
        away.
My mind thirsted
    for knowledge,
    and you were
        as a greedy desert.
Oh where were
    you Mary, Charles—
    that you could not hear.
My heart broke,
    and my universe
        rioted and screamed,
Yet you were deaf,
        or, perhaps,
My heart was mute.
Oh Val, Michael, Jane,
    If you would but
    speak and release
        me from my spell,
And inwardly I died,
    and you could have
        saved me,
But you would not hear.
Oh Lord,
    how many
        souls have
cried out to me,
    and I have
not heard
        or
refused to hear,
and so, condemned us all
to die inside?

YVETTE JOHNSON

Yvette Johnson, twenty-seven years old, was born in Annapolis, Maryland, and attended public school in Baltimore. She received her B.A degree in English from Coppin State College in Baltimore, and is employed as a Caseworker with the Baltimore City Department of Social Service.

GHETTO

Having reached my boiling point
I overrun my container
Flowing over and out,
Leaving my mark
On everything I touch.

REALITY

A bare uncovered bulb
Casting shadows on the wall
Creating monsters from the unknown—
Lighting up my failures;
Pointing out my inadequacies;
Making me face reality;—
Until I pull the string.

SAPLING

Allotted a four-by-four square,
set out all alone
to depend on nature or
the goodness of man
for your nourishment:
as you look down
cold winds sweep the day's
living past you,
and you're left on your own
to grow straight—tall;
to fall prey to disease;
to grow crooked—fall.

THIS IS THE CITY

Kids in the street
Playing kick the can;
Can't take a street shower—
There's a water ban.
Knots of people milling on corners.
Partial remains of a hopscotch game.
Trash-littered asphalt streets . . . . .
Does anyone care?

DAVID LLORENS

David Llorens, thirty years old, is Associate Editor of *Ebony Magazine*. His poems, essays, articles and reviews have appeared in numerous periodicals and anthologies. Presently he is a visiting lecturer in Black Literature and Consultant to the Committee on Black Studies at the University of Washington.

A RESONANT SILENCE

Do you also hear the silence between us?
And you and me like slippers,
Still, though once
we danced.

Perhaps the music was not quite in tune,
And the joy, a fleeting one.
Yet, it is a truth
We shared

Now the sorrow whenever our eyes must meet,
Wondering who is to blame.
But simply said
We needed.

And how might mortals measure distance
Of roads yet unwalked.
So sweet the way
We tried.

So let us together claim our innocence,
Knowing we meant no ill.
Saying to time,
We lived.

Like memories, the silence is no less ours,
And if it speaks of hurt,
Perhaps that means
We loved.

WAYWARD CHILD

The bearded one sees the joy
On the faces of his brothers and sisters
As they boogaloo.
"Doesn't manhood mean anything to them," he wonders.
Feet moving everywhere artistically
Remind him that his poetry is not without flaw.
Nobody doubts that the enemy
Cannot outdo them at their chosen pace
While the bearded one senses
A death in his choice because
The form he uses is more ambiguous
Than their dance
And less sure than the razor.
So intense this saviour's need
To awaken them to his peculiar pain
That often he forgets that their way
Is not painless.

DOC LONG, JR.

Doughtry Long, Jr. ("Doc Long"), twenty-six years old, was born in Atlanta, Georgia. He lived for two years in Africa, and has traveled in the Virgin Islands and throughout the Southern United States. The poems offered here are excerpts from a collection to be published in early 1970 by Broadside Press.

#4

Where my grandmother lived
there was always sweet potato pie
and thirds on green beans and
songs and words of how we'd
survived it all.
Blackness.
And the wind
a soft lull
in the pecan tree
whispered
Ethiopia
        Ethiopia, Ethiopia
E-th-io-piaaaaa!

#20

from the window
the moment is a bird
against cool
            winter skies
and trees naked in the wind;
I move from it thinking of you
brown and ready,
then tremble with summerness.

#25

if 'Trane had only seen
                    her body
and the way it smoothed
                    the brown light and
sent color to
the edge of darkness
as if it were the perfect
hands of some painter
he would have named it
with his horn;
                    something vibrant and
unexplored something loud
and still as someone
first touching their blackness.

#28

Black people
have got to be Black
or sleep
into a dying
and forget
that each of them is a sun-god
we've gotta listen
the chaos around us is deep

BARBARA MARSHALL

Barbara Marshall, twenty-five years old, was born and educated in Maryland. She has taught dance and dance drama. Presently she is fellowship student at Antioch Putney Graduate School.

COLONIZED MIND

Say you, brother!
Congratulations!
What a fine job you've done
Teaching the true history to everyone.

Brothers and sisters,
Getting together
Examining a past of truth
Assembling an ideology for the temporal youth.

Your classes
Are charismatic!
My, that makes me feel good inside!—
As brilliant as the colorful dashiki-cladded pride.

You've penetrated
Existential psychosis;
Painted new images, man!—
Telling of kingdoms past in our motherland.

Wait—brother!
About an instant ago—
What kind of images did you imbibe?
To down a brother with a forty-five?

LITTLE BLACK BOY

Little black boy
With eyes so curious,
Whose lips form a question,
Give me your hand.
Let me feel your clasp.
The sound of your tiny feet
Pattering along cemented walks
And stumbling yet on littered ways
Is so reminiscent.
And you are making wishes—
You're saturated with countless wishes—
So many wishes!
Don't fret, brown-eyed chap!
Proud black men have died,
Shall die and will kill,
To deliver and fulfill your dreams!

ON PHILOSOPHY

The Lawd is dead,
White men philosophize.
"Ain't so," the black man quips,
"No need to eulogize."

The black continued with his wiry charm.
"Niggers been askin' for so much," he replied,
"The weary Lawd just got a notion
To run away and hide."

REQUEST

When you chart your course
May I tag along?
Just a little comma,
Indeed
An effervescent comforter.
Will you heighten my crescendo
With an exclamation point—?

HERMAN L. McMILLAN

Herman McMillan, twenty-nine years old, has spent most of his life in reform schools, where he began reading poetry, psychology, and philosophy "to pass the time." He has been in prison for the past ten years, where he divides his time between writing with the hope of publication and writing briefs pleading for his release.

EQUALITY

We all
came screaming into the world—
but there the sameness ends
with the

cut in—
to myriad facets and
pigmentation's many
colors

LOOKING FOR EQUALITY

I search
the iridescent faces
met in this partial world
looking

for you,
equality. In biased
hearts I found abstract nouns
like love.

each thought
his own intangible kind
supremely different
from mine.

LOST LOVE

In autumn
the barren trees'
empty arms
plead summer's
return.

NOCTURNAL

Night drops
within black America
blackness of poverty
erupts.

false gay
fun in dipsomania
crescendos from black throats.
empty

black heads
nod in euphoria-sleep
vainly to fill their void.
bodies

monkey
dance with infectious madness,
jerk in rhythmic spasms.
groovy

black souls
pulsate from motown sound tracts—
neurotic wails and riffs
wake dawn

CAROLYN J. OGLETREE

Carolyn J. Ogletree, twenty-one years old, studied Architecture at Tuskegee Institute, and is now attending San Francisco State College. Her paintings have been exhibited at the Spectrum Gallery in Oakland, California. She hopes to attend the University of Stockholm (Sweden) in 1970.

FORMULA

I want you to *stop, think* and say a prayer
When things begin to get you down
And the world keeps going round and round
Stop, think and say a prayer
When your heart is heavy
and your load is hard to bear
Stop, think and say a prayer
When the day just won't go right
And you find yourself getting all uptight
Stop and look around you and say *God Bless*
One silent prayer is better
Than a bag full of sorrows
It might even keep you friends
For a brighter tomorrow .   .   .

LIFE IS THE ART OF DRAWING

Life is the art of drawing
Lines, oil, paint and chalk
Red, white and blue
America

Life is the art of drawing
Brushes, pencil on canvas
Red, white and blue
America

Life is the art of drawing
From bed to bed and room to room
Red, white and blue
America

Life is the art of drawing
Boy, girl, marriage
Saint Mary's church
Red, white and blue
America

Life is the art of drawing
House, car and society
Red, white and blue
America

Life is the art of drawing
5, 4, 3, 2, 1, children—P.T.A.
Red, white and blue
America

Life is the art of drawing
Black and white, no harmony
Red, white and blue
America

Life is the art of drawing
Wars and countless deaths
Red, white and blue
America

Life is the art of drawing
Peace
Red, white and blue
America

DANIEL W. OWENS

Daniel Walter Owens, twenty-one years old, is a native of Massachusetts. He is married, and is attending the University of Massachusetts at Boston. He is one of three resident playwrights for the new African Theatre Company of Boston. Two of his plays were produced during the summer of 1969.

BORNE

Borne across rivers of grey, life forces
pulsating, gushing to 'n fro, never overflowing
their banks, escaping their channels;

Borne over mountains strewn with ashes, black
souls "never got over," the Phoenix is a
Blackhawk—not a crow called jim—

Borne thru vales, a mist of sweat tinged red,
enshrouding shot-up, shot-down lives, stinging
flesh flayed by hate.....racism.........;

Born to live.....to die.....to be BLACK.....

HENRIETTA C. PARKS

Henrietta C. Parks is nineteen years old. A freshman at San Diego State College, she hopes to become a psychologist or a social worker. She writes "I am trying to be somebody and I hope someone will give me the chance."

MY LIFE

The stars by night are the candles which light up my soul;
The prayer I pray today turns the pages of my life,
And God is my home and my salvation.
The time I spent today is only a speck in the hour glass;
My time is about due and I hope I'll be ready.

UNCERTAINTY

To walk in the muck of uncertainty
And only existing in the slime of despair
And yet reaching for a firm hold
Only to lose the grip of certainty
Then asking where do I go from there?
How can I reach and really give?
Then it happens!
The hand each of us needs appears before me
From this I draw my strength
The happening one seeks
The flower.

DOROTHY C. PARRISH

Dorothy C. Parrish, twenty-seven years old, received her A.B. degree in Political Science. She has appeared in several Ed Bullins' plays. She has been writing for several years, but has not published before. At present she is living and working in San Francisco.

you made me a slave and kept me a slave
through the oh say can you see normal and
orderly democratic processes of the land of
the free; you gave me jim crow you beat me
and lynched me without interference from
the star spangled normal and orderly demo-
cratic processes of the home of the brave;
you enfeebled my brain you made me a
pauper a beggar who could only look for-
ward to the next pitiful dole you offered
through the what so proudly we hailed
normal and orderly democratic processes;
—and now you vow to right your oh say
does that star spangled banner yet wave
wrongs if only i will wait through the twi-
lights last gleaming, because it takes time
to achieve the rockets red glare the bombs
bursting in air and such a massive domestic
task o'er the land of the normal and orderly
democratic processes

HUSH NOW

Hush now baby, not a peep—
Don't you fret now; no, don't weep.
Wait now baby, not so fast—
If you cry, the dream won't last.

Black child! Black child! Can't you see?
you lie in the cradle of liberty!
See it there child
  Freedom waits!
Just beyond those pearl white gates.

Hurry now child
Run, be quick!
The plague has spread
The babe is sick.
The germ is there
Human fires ignited—
Black men grow now
  Freedom's sighted!

INDICTMENT

Shame on you!
You promised to be
The Land of the Free despite your
Uh—peculiar institution.

Shame on you!
You hid all my glory
Belied my great story
Shame, Shame on you!

SOLILOQUY

Loneliness lies just there beyond heartbreak
Happiness lies over there, far away.
I am between—
Not alone,
Not with others—
I am here.

ANTOINETTE T. PAYNE

Antoinette Theresa Payne, twenty years old, is a junior at Queens College, New York, majoring in Sociology and Anthropology. In the summer of 1967 she studied at the University of Madrid, and traveled through Northern Spain, London, Holland, and Paris.

OH! LORD

Please Lord, take care of my child;—
my child with the heavy eye brows,
and the look of despair.
"Follow the way of God, children,
for it is a difficult road to freedom.

"Climb the highest mountain,
look across the longest waterway,—
to find it's only a mole hill,
and a pond you can never cross."

My child is living a life,
bound in chains;
chains wrapped around his body
chains never ceasing . . . always tightening
with every movement.

Please Lord, take my child into your bosom,
and smother him, so he won't see
the pain and anguish of his mother.
Blind his eyes, oh Lord.
Let him see nothing but darkness until
the sun rays reflect the love of mankind.
Then—and only then—oh Lord,
let him see.

HELEN G. QUIGLESS

Helen G. Quigless, twenty-five years old, is a native of Washington, D. C. Her poems have been published in several anthologies and periodicals. Presently, she is Media Specialist at Federal City College, Washington, D. C.

AT THE EBONY CIRCLE

They came to catch the stars
on a rainy night.

Red swirls of light danced
through the room of shadows
as one's favorite beer
appeared again, again.

As she leaned, mirrors in the cigarette
machine reflected
multi-images of her "afro."

He brushed past
her and
there was not
much room between.

Around the round tables
the ebony circles,   night
filled faces flexed and
passionately gleamed.

At the circle's edge
others witnessed from faces
of precious glass

as music pounded hardened
echoes into their heads, and voices

"I am my own self."

"You are my own woman."

"Call me by my rightful name!"

—and voices mingled
with the clanking stars
in tall frosty glasses.

                  in the rain,
The Shining Moon Was Black.

CIRCLED BY A HORSEFLY

Guns and knives aren't enough.
What does one do when circled
by a horsefly?

Day by day the horror increases.
Will all Black Americans suddenly
Be Killed?   With their
eyes WIDE open?

When they took Martin—they showed us what
they think.

black men are not

My advice:

Assume a state of anxiety
in which one is on constant
alert for defense
. . . for defense (mind you)
. . . for defense.
And apply daily,
a lot of bug spray.

LIP SERVICE

The words, "eye"
"close, and open"—
arms stretching the length of argument;
I'm watching
the words
the words
why does his head
angle above the statement?

EUGENE REDMOND

Eugene Redmond, thirty years old, is Poet-in-Residence and Director of Language workshops at Southern Illinois University's Experiment in Higher Education. His work has been published in numerous publications and in the anthology *The New Black Poetry* and will be included in "*A GALAXY OF BLACK WRITING*" to be published shortly.

EVANESCENT LOVE

I gazed sadly from my window
Onto the quiet murmur and peace
Of October treetops,
And saw amidst the lively greens
A fast-dying oak, all nude and grey.

I saw the red-green grass below
Play zig-zag on the earth's tan basin;
And those fleeting strands of life
Made me strangely alone.

A dying love—the lonely tree seemed,
Aged and worn from time's harsh mold;
And if, I thought, life and love are
One, then life and love are gone.

RUSH CITY—THE HOLE

Tottering brick volcanoes
Exhume smoke from the rust-red
Bellies of iron furnaces;
The jaws are wooden hulks
That lean; the eyes glass
With old rags stuffed around
Them; the nostrils hingeless
Doors batted down by an invisible
Demon, cold, evil and furiously driven.
Through the eyes Black faces
Peer out on the hole surrounded
By railroad tracks and a river—
The color of dung.

In summer pigeons fly out
From two Black bridges that
Slice the hole; and
Workmen sneer down on marble games and yell
Fifty cents offers
To little girls unfamiliar with themselves.
Beset mornings by
A caravan of foreigners,
The city each evening
Takes stock of its losses:
Lapsed insurance policies, non-breakable
Dishes that break, heads bloodied by
The cop's stick, death
Of the sick waiting for an ambulance,
Paper houses cut into by blades of flame
Before the fire engine clears the firehouse doors,
The uncollared dog
Taken to the soap factory.

The way out is ALWAYS up
For people without wings;

And the sun trudges slowly
From State Street where day
Prevails when the hole is dark,
And it is then that
Eyes peer out ahead of kerosene
Lamps and 30-Watt bulbs.

SPRING IN THE JUNGLE

You tiptoed
Naked
Into the
Jungle
Of my soul;

And the underbrush
Divided before
You.

A choir of birds
Grew
Understandably
Silent;

And I stood
Beside
Myself with joy
And watched
The season grow
To
Spring.

Let my soul
Be always
Green
And sprinkled with
Daisies;

Let there be
Dew for sun to bathe in
And winds to do rituals
For the Moon.

ROBERT REEDBURG

Robert Reedburg, twenty-nine years old, has published poetry in numerous periodicals and newspapers. He was cited as Best Poet of the Studio Watts Festival of the Performing Arts for his poem. "Epitaph to A Man."

EPITAPH TO A MAN

In memory of Dr. Martin Luther King, Jr.

The Lord made clay of spittle and
anointed my eyes and I went and I
in God (Juan 9: 11).
washed and I saw and I have believed

What moved you Martin
who directed your course?
why cleanse America
of an unjust source?

I'm going to sit
at the welcome table
one of these days

With talents like yours
you had it made
you could have rested
in the do-nothing shade

Strange
men are called
from every path
not knowing or caring
of destiny's wrath

MONTGOMERY

We rode the dusty bus

BIRMINGHAM

We marched
though clubs cracked skulls

and bigots made democracy
and equality— a plaything

JACKSON

Poor black mothers scorned
beaten, kicked, jailed
victims of hate
created by an ungrateful society

WASHINGTON

We marched with dignity
black and white
together
America was unashamed

Tens of thousands
led by the
grandson of a slave

I'm going to sit
at the welcome table
one of these days

What moved you Martin
who directed your course?
why cleanse America
of an unjust source?

Move along train
you got
a heavy load . . .

Weaker men tried
none could succeed
black men heard you
answered your pleas

No,
not just black men Martin
your strength came from
the hearts of all men
freedom and justice
have no color

My country 'tis of thee
my country 'tis of thee
sweet land of liberty
sweet land of liberty

On the dirt roads of Georgia
let freedom ring
in the squalid ghettos of Harlem
let freedom ring

Wherever men
have cause to be
let freedom ring

Fate
moved you Martin
God directed your course
to cleanse America
of an unjust source

Black and white
together
we shall overcome
someday . . .

Move along train
you got
a heavy load . . .

Save all your dreams

wrap them in the velvet
carpet of life

I'm going to sit
at the welcome table
one of these days

Free at last!
free at last!
thank God Almighty!
I'm free at last!. . . . . .

Rest In Peace. . . .

YESTERDAY'S CHILD

As a youth
I knew the venom of Watts
the pangs of its poverty
crushed me into nothing

I grew on frustration
misunderstanding
a thousand Saturdays
Christmas was . . .

Mama
prepared for each Sunday
chicken was
never too good for us

Awed
I watched
the hostile passengers
aboard the mighty red car

An animal
in a cage was I
left to eat
from the cancer
called home

As a youth
I knew the venom of Watts
with its roach infested
housing projects

Young girls
flirting with motherhood
today we live
tomorrow we die

Christ
in store fronts
Christ
on a cross
what can he buy?
tomorrow is mother's day . . .

I knew the anger of hope
Labor Day, Christmas, Easter
Lend me
your New Year

As a youth
I knew the fire of the Holy Ghost
welfare lines, insurance men
bill collectors, society's scapegoats

First class, second class
who am I?
yesterday's child, preferably denied
oppressed, justice perverted

As a youth
I knew lies, promises
Christmas
was always coming

Facts obscured
talk, social discord
prayer
crushed by the snake

Pacified
by my brother
the keeper;
time of fury, action

I am no stranger
I cry for America
I grieve for
Yesterday's child. . . .

CAROLYN M. RODGERS

Carolyn M. Rodgers, twenty-eight years old, lives in Chicago. The two poems published here are from her collection, *Songs of A Blackbird*. She is also author of *2 Love Raps* published by Third World Press.

U NAME THIS ONE

let the r(evolution) come. uh
state of peace is not known to me
anyway
since i grew uhround in chi town
where
howlin wolf howled in the tavern on 47th st.
and muddy waters made you cry the salty nigger
blues,
  where pee wee cut lonnell fuh messin wid
  his sistuh; and blood baptized the street
  at least twice every week and judy got
  kicked outa grammar school fuh bein pregnant
  and died tryin to ungrow the seed
    we was all up in there and
    ev'ryday was guerilla warfare, yeah.

let uh r(evolution) come
couldn't be no
action
like what i dun already
seen.

WE DANCE LIKE ELLA RIFFS

the room was a
red, glow, there was
a warm close pulsating.
chairs and tables were
               sprawled alike a semi-circle
bowing to the bandstand where
                   ripples of light lingered
on the silver tracings of player's
soulpieces and
brightened and glistened and
dazzjangled
like tear drops
cornered
       suspended
and spit on by the light
             again and again and oooooohweeee
              (splu dah dee
              do dah 'um dah
              spleeeeeeee
the dancers were
soft breezes, smooth
jerky moving
balloon move the air
roll with the notes
sift through the beats
seep, the music
           sure carelessly careful, caresses cor-recting
           the air

             du-wahhhhhhhhhhh
we is music
sound motion imitate
each is us
Black variations
          on a

Round   /   theme
any one
of us—
an infinite, essential note
                    sounding down this world

LINWOOD D. SMITH

Linwood Daggette Smith, Jr., twenty-six years old, is a graduate of Howard University and Gallaudet College for the Hard of Hearing. He is a teacher for the Deaf and Blind at Governor Morehead School in Raleigh, North Carolina. His poetry has been published in various magazines, and newspapers, and he is now preparing a book collection for publication.

DAWN SONG

This morning at seven
The siren of a police car
Was my alarm clock.

FREE WINE ON COMMUNION DAY

✼ ✼ ✼ ✼ ✼ ✼ ✼

Rev. Malcolm Lassiter
Tantown Church of God:
"Through these doors, pass flocks
Of the blackest sheep in the world . . .
And for them . . . I offer, no water
But free wine on communion day . . ."

✼ ✼ ✼ ✼ ✼ ✼ ✼

Mrs. Washington:
When I get up to heaven
I ain't gonna work no more,
Forget how to polish silver
How to scrub and wax a floor.

No more "yessing and no mamming"
I'm gonna get away from it all,
Gonna sit on the right hand of Jesus
And have no worries a'tall.
I heard about the good times in heaven
For all the trouble you have on earth,
And you can bet your barrel of pig feet
I'm gonna get my two cents worth.

PRIDE AND PREJUDICE

Last week . . . I heard a man speak . . .
It shamed me that he knew a lot more
About Martin Luther King and CORE,
The Negro and the Jew
Than I did. He spoke eloquently
About Adam Clayton Powell, SNCC,
A. Phillip Randolph and H. Rap Brown's
Syndrome of burning America down.
Stokely Carmichael, Bayard Rustin
The myth of the Negro's "leering and lustin'"

(How well this White man understood
The source and meaning of Brotherhood.)

The novels of Baldwin, the poetry of Hughes
Rose into his subterfuge.
His speech reached me deep inside
Until it drew out all my pride,
And when he came into the end
I wondered . . .
                    would he be my friend?

WHAT GOOD ARE WORDS?

For Martin Luther King

Behold, here cometh the dreamer,
let us slay him, and we shall see
what will become of his dreams.
Genesis 37:   19–20

What good are words to quench a heart on fire?
What good are words to halt dreams unfulfilled?
What good are words to stifle people's ire,
When a member of their family is killed?
He had a dream, a dream of faith and hope
But what's a dream if it cannot come true?
He had a dream to which we should aspire,
One America for me and you.
What good are words if they cannot change
Attitudes of those who foster hate?
What good are words if they can't rearrange
The crooked man and make him turn out straight?

His loss is ours, his dream our legacy
One America . . . for you and me.

Non-violence, was his plan for freedom
This was the thing, he thought was best,
To win equality for his and for all people
And at the same time banish bitterness.
This was his dream, but now his dream is gone
It was to us, to whom his torch was thrown,
What shall become of his dream of faith
Do we have strength to make his dream our own?

His loss is ours, his dream our legacy
An America in which we ALL are FREE!

CHARLES STEWART

Charles Stewart, twenty-five years old, is a native New Yorker. He is currently an English Major at Manhattan College, and hopes eventually to teach English on the high school level.

THIS IS FOR FREEDOM, MY SON

Put on that uniform, my son.
What for, Father?
You are going to fight for your country, my son.
But Father, I am black and I want to go to college!
My son, you can go to college when you return
And your color doesn't matter; you are going to fight
For the freedom of all people.

That's it, Son, line that Swastika up, now set it
right on top of the sight; that's it Son, get that
Rising sun right between the eyes, squeeze gently
my son, squeeze gently.
But Father, you taught me not to kill!
This is different; this is for freedom, my son.

That's it Son, you loosen the pins so they come out
easy; now when those Hammers and Sickles start up
the hill, you pull out the pins and roll these down
to meet them.
But why am I over here doing this Father? I want to
go home.
It is necessary that you be over here, this is
for freedom, my son.

The next time you see the flash Son, you take a
reading, and someone over there in "D" company
sector will be doing the same thing. Now where
these lines meet on the chart is where they will
drop the napalm.
But why should I do this Father?
This is for freedom . . .
No Father, that's not what I meant; why should the air
force get all the glory? When it gets dark I'll
stalk him and light him up with my M15.
Very good, you learn well, my son.

Father, it's so good to be home again.
Yes my son, now get over in this line.
What for, Father?
We are going to picket my son, do you know the song
that we sing? Now sing with me—We shall overcome . . .
But why am I doing this Father?
This is for freedom, my son.

ROBERT J. SYE

Robert J. Sye, thirty years old, was born in Texas. He has worked as Editor of the *San Francisco Sun*—Reporter and Entertainment Editor of the *Los Angeles Sentinel*. Presently, he is heading "the first black Public Relations firm in Hollywood."

WHY I REBEL

I rebel
Not because of poverty,
Joblessness, ghettoization, bias, or hot summers
But to remind the Nation
of its dishonesty, injustices,
Apathetic legislation, and civil indifference.

I rebel
For it's a catalyst
That flames the conscience;
I rebel
For it explodes the Atom
of a discontented black people
In anguished quest
Of a new Emancipation, one
That's not ambiguous rhetoric
But judicial, plainly humanistic,
And, cogent; complete with
All the "inalienable rights"
That God and the Constitution
Accorded man—black and white.

I rebel
Because it's a positive reactant
That resuscitates a dying society
And makes it taste, feel, see the ugly evidences
Of animated fury and dissatisfaction,
Of needed changes—
In housing, in economic equalization
In philosophy, in job opportunity,
And, in ideas.

I rebel
Because he (the white man) has humiliated me
More than any diabolical demon

Burning in the fiery abyss of hell could have;
And with Satanic cunning he severed,
For more than four hundred years, along with
My umbilical cord, my dignity, honor, and a part
Of my heritage.

Now he rages, enacts laws
In (sheer)
Desperation
In panic-stricken funk,
In white-livered cowardice.
Now he blames, persecutes the Rap Browns,
The Floyd McKissicks, and the Stokely Carmichaels.
Anyone who aggregates black unity.

I rebel
Not to be defiant, or recusant
But to make society
Cognizant that I am.

VALERIE TARVER

Valerie Tarver, fourteen years old, is in the ninth grade of junior high school. A member of the National Junior Honor Society, and recipient of several awards in public speaking, art, and Black culture, she hopes to go into the fields of Sociology and Political Science.

DIFFERENCES

Live and love; live and love.
I am a hawk; or I am a dove;
I am the wind; I am the sea;
Your skin is white; mine is black;
And, don't you see
If it makes a difference to you,
Then it makes a difference to me.
I am the sun; I am the earth;
A product of my Creator.
I am as good as you;—
You are as good as me.
Why can't I love you?
Why DON'T you love me?

EXPLANATION

I don't hate your color
I only hate your actions and deeds.
I hate you for giving me
All the terrible reasons to hate.

"I PLEDGE ALLEGIANCE"

I pledge allegiance to a false symbol—
The biggest lie ever told;
The saddest promises ever broken.
Yet you call it a "good example!"
"Liberty or death"
"Land of the free"
"Old Glory"
Yeah, you know those familiar phrases,
Patriotic words to a nation
That commits treason upon itself.

"White stars for justice,"
That's a lie! a lie!
"White stripes for equality"—
For which my brothers have to die;
Die for promises made but never backed.
I've gotten used to you white man
Doctor, government official, law man
Or whatever you may be.
Telling the truth is something that you've always lacked.
Red stripes for the blood my brothers shed.
In the war, in the ghetto streets
In the little Jim Crow country town.
The blood of a man; for you he bleeds, for you he bleeds
The Black man whom you don't even want to feed.
Blue squares for lies—and more;—
Yeah, this country is free with a closed door!

You gave us liberty instead of death
And you want to give me laws
and commandments which you never kept
And say it's my problem!
Do you expect me to bow my head and solve it?
No! I will fight—until you give me liberty;
Until you give me my rights.

TO THE WHITE MAN

Well, white man, are you confused?
Are you wondering what's happening
To your polite little black boy?
Are you confused, white man,
Because he no longer wants to hold your hand;
Because he wants to stand on his own two feet,
Not on a white crutch?

Are you confused because he no longer
Wants to slave and toil for you?
Because he wants to work and till his own soil?
Are you confused, white man, because black
Is now positive, no longer negative?

Are you confused because black man
Has now found beauty within himself,—
A beauty that has always been there,
But no one succeeded in pushing you
Aside to turn on the light?

White man, are you confused because
You don't quite know how to approach
This human of burning hatred and pride
Who wants to stand up and shine—
Not run away and hide?

WHY are you confused, white man?

AUSTIN D. WASHINGTON

Austin D. Washington, twenty-seven years old, is a native of Durham, North Carolina. He has received B.A. and M.A. degrees in History from the University of North Carolina at Durham. Presently, he is a graduate student in History at the Pennsylvania State University.

TO BE BLACK IS TO SUFFER

To be black is to suffer:—
Suffer—Suffer—Suffer.
Martin Luther King—unredemptive suffering;
W. E. B. DuBois—unparalleled suffering;
Malcolm X—provocative suffering;
You and me—collective suffering.
To be black is to suffer, suffer, suffer.
So suffer!—suffer!—suffer!

TOMMY WHITAKER

Tommy Whitaker, twenty years old, was born in Vicksburg, Mississippi. He started writing at the age of thirteen. A collection of his poetry will be published soon by Broadside Press. He joined the Air Force in 1968, and in August 1969 was stationed in Thailand.

AFTER DEPRESSION CAME SOUL

When you see me walkin'
singin'
with my diddy-bop walk,
you say i got soul,
i got rhythm.
i even heard you say
"look at that BROTHER, he got Soul, man!"
But one of my deepest wishes
is to see a pair of eyes
that knew the color of the unborn
that took in nourishments
which produced
soul rhythm.

First, there was depression;
then came soul.
So next time
you see me walkin'
singin'
it may be best
to step
aside.

ONE WAY

You!
the great America.
                shooting
for the stars;
the moon:
anxious to leave
the blind
                behind.
"Why not?" you say.
but
during next
blastoff
i've planned—to go
along.

WARNER B. WIMS

Warner B. Wims, twenty-four years old, lives in Syracuse, New York, where he serves as Director of Counseling at the Cooperative College Center. He has traveled throughout the country recruiting blacks for higher education, dispersing information about campus underground activities, and studying black student unrest.

THE PAINFUL QUESTION

The question is
whether or not I can allow myself to hang dangling
before the open mouth of a glutton
and risk slipping and falling into a grave which could
have at least been marked

the answer is that I must disallow the staff
of waiting for some unknown god to step in and
lift the giant's finger backward and release me
from his grasp to let me know what being free means

the answer is that I must rip the strings
but find the cord which was once tied, then cut,
by the baracoons and hoe

the answer is that: I can't wait until the next child
finds its number and sets aside a coffin at eight; to
steal and hide until it's too late to steal and hide some more.

A biographical note about the editor, with a sampling of some of her poems.

BEATRICE M. MURPHY

Beatrice M. Murphy (Mrs. Beatrice Murphy Campbell) has edited two previous anthologies: *Negro Voices* and *Ebony Rhythm;* has published a book of her own poetry, *Love Is a Terrible Thing,* a "how-to" pamphlet for writers, *Catching the Editor's Eye,* and with Dr. Nancy Arnez, a pamphlet of poetry, *The Rocks Cry Out.* Presently she is Director of The Negro Bibliographic and Research Center, Inc., and Managing Editor of its publication *Bibliographic Survey: The Negro in Print.*

WE PASS

Let the leaders of nations
Who sit in sheltered places
Haranguing the state of the world
And pronouncing as their conclusion
That "war is inevitable"
Fight the next one.

Let them pull their fat thighs
Out of soft, easy chairs,
And march off to the cold
The wet, the filth that is war
To fight the next one.

Let them cower and find no hiding place
From terror in the skies.
Let them sweat out peace negotiations
Bereft of arms—of legs—of sight;
Bereft of futures they fought to secure.

Too old? They are not too old.
No man is ever too old to die;
Only too young; too young to lie
Face up, unseeing and alone
On foreign soil; To have his life
Snuffed out before it has begun;
Before he has known love,
Happiness and fulfillment.

Let the leaders of nations
Who ponder the state of the world
And make the final pronouncements
Fight their "inevitable wars"
But let them leave our sons at home.

EVICTED

Huddled there on the sidewalk is heartbreak.
Broken, soiled pieces of furniture;
Faded, tattered articles of clothing;
The epitome of one man's hell,
How could a cynic observer know
The stories all these could tell—
Not just of strivings—frustrations—
Want and despair; but of dreams—
Ambitions—deep love and fulfillment—
All buried now in defeat, and the
Belongings huddled forlornly there.

TRIVIA

Such trivial things
You stop to argue!
Is God black or white?
What difference does it make?
I saw two children come
Laughing down the street
Hair flying and arms entwined.
One was blond with blue eyes
Shining like the morning sun;
One was black with dark eyes
Sparkling like a diamond mine.
I stood and watched their faces;
And when I was done, knew that I
Had seen the smile of God
In each one.

8-41
49-64
67-95